MODERN JAZZ BASS EXERCISES & ETUDES

The Complete Method to Develop Technique, Harmonic Knowledge & Creativity On Jazz Bass

JOHN PATITUCCI

FUNDAMENTAL CHANGES

Modern Jazz Bass Exercises & Etudes

The Complete Method to Develop Technique, Harmonic Knowledge & Creativity On Jazz Bass

ISBN: 978-1-78933-452-4

Published by **www.fundamental-changes.com**

Copyright © 2025 John Patitucci

Edited by Tim Pettingale

www.fundamental-changes.com

Join our free Facebook Community of Cool Musicians

www.facebook.com/groups/fundamentalguitar

For over 350 free guitar lessons with Videos, check out:

www.fundamental-changes.com

Transcription and notation by Johnny Cox

https://johnnycoxmusic.com

Cover Image Copyright: Author photo, used by permission.

Contents

Introduction

Over the years, whenever students have struggled with specific areas of their bass playing, my response has been to write an exercise or etude that directly addresses the problem. I have dozens of these filed away and in this book I've compiled the most effective studies that have helped my students' playing the most.

This book is organized into three sections:

- Technical Drills

- Fretboard Knowledge

- Diminished, Whole Tone, Augmented Sounds & Tetrachords

The drills focus on training specific skills that, over time, we want to become automatic for us. Technique is just the means by which we make music, and the better our technical skills, the easier it is for us to play the music we hear in our head. Our goal is to be able to focus on making great music without being hampered or distracted by technical issues in our playing. So, these exercises set out to refine the most important areas of technique.

The fretboard knowledge section contains etudes concerned with how we apply our technique in music making, and are an important means of improving our fretboard visualization.

If, for example, we are asked to play a series of arpeggios moving through the Circle of Fifths, with the additional challenge of connecting each arpeggio via the next nearest available note, that will test both our ability to *see* the arpeggios mapped across the fretboard *and* our string crossing technique.

While the first two sections focus on technique and fretboard visualization with some musical application, the third section is dedicated to dealing with some of the advanced harmonic techniques currently being used in modern jazz.

In summary, this collection of studies will develop your bass playing in the following areas:

- **Tone production** – whether playing an exercise or a musical etude, our focus will always be on producing a great tone

- **Timing** – all the studies here should be practiced with a metronome or over a drum groove. Great time and great tone are two of the biggest assets any bass player can have. Possessing these qualities is much more important than clever harmonic knowledge

- **Interval recognition** – a great benefit of drilling triads, arpeggios, and scales is growing the skill of being able to hear a specific interval and immediately locate it on the fretboard. This will help every aspect of your bass playing, including comping or soloing over changes

- **Fretboard knowledge** – as we work with specific patterns on the fretboard – major 9 arpeggios, for example – our fretboard knowledge will grow organically. This is a musically satisfying way to increase our mastery of the fretboard

- **Rhythm reading** – many of the exercises and etudes here deliberately include rhythmic elements designed to challenge your reading and playing skills. Whether it's a passage arranged in 1/8th note triplets, combined with 1/16th note syncopation, or another approach, your understanding of rhythms and your ability to read them will improve

- **Technical execution** – every exercise will help to refine your technical ability. Smooth string crossing, for instance, is an area of technique we can never spend too much time on. Here, we'll sometimes work on technique in a focused way, and other times it will happen organically as we play melodic etudes that rely on certain techniques

- **Advanced harmonic techniques** – Last, but not least, I felt it was important to include some focused work on diminished, augmented, whole tone and hexatonic concepts, which will help to expand your harmonic knowledge and open up new sounds to you

One final piece of advice: developing speed is not a goal of this book. I want you to learn to play these exercises and etudes cleanly, with great time, tone and feel. It's important to train your muscle memory really well to create a solid foundation for your playing, so take your time and focus on quality.

Finally, the audio examples in this book were played by my friend and bass transcriber Johnny Cox. The reason I asked Johnny to do it is, the point of these exercises and etudes is to find *your* voice and point of view on bass. The point is not to play them like me! My desire is that you'll sound like *you*, and develop these ideas according to your own personal style and sound.

Now, let's get started, and I hope you find lots of valuable material for your practice sessions!

John

Get the Audio

The audio files for this book are available to download for free from **www.fundamental-changes.com.** The link is in the top right-hand corner. Click on the Bass link then simply select this book title from the drop-down menu and follow the instructions to get the audio.

We recommend that you download the files directly to your computer, not to your tablet, and extract them there before adding them to your media library. On the download page there are instructions, and we also provide technical support via the contact form.

For over 350 free guitar lessons with videos check out:

www.fundamental-changes.com

Join our free Facebook Community of Cool Musicians

www.facebook.com/groups/fundamentalguitar

Tag us for a share on Instagram: **FundamentalChanges**

Part 1 – Technical Drills

1. Thirds Workout

This technical drill is based around the idea of playing 3rd intervals in 1/8th notes. It serves as a useful warm-up that makes use of the full range of a four-string electric bass.

Play this exercise slowly to begin with, using a metronome set to 100bpm, and get a feel for how it moves across the fretboard. Begin to increase the tempo in small increments as you become more confident.

The note pattern and the use of rests here are deliberately varied, and the exercise is long enough so that you don't simply memorize it. Instead, focus on reading the rhythms and playing each phrase as cleanly and evenly as possible with great tone.

Exercise 1

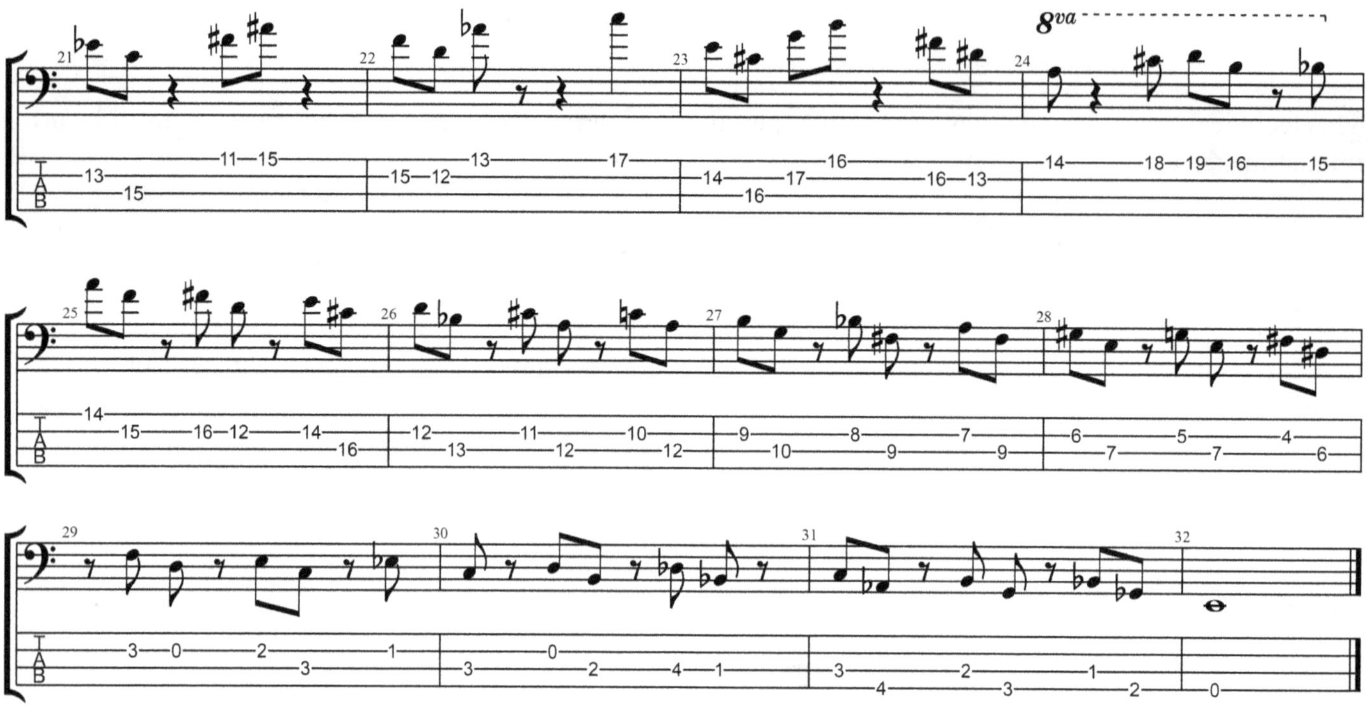
8va

2. String Crossing – Part 1

This exercise is the first of a series of drills focusing on the all-important skill of string crossing. This drill is based around first position on the bass. I originally wrote the exercise based around the *half position* on double bass, which corresponds to the first three frets on an electric bass. However, electric bassists will generally play the first four or even five frets as their "first position", so the drill has been adapted accordingly.

Exercise 2 shows the basic shape of the exercise. We're crossing from one string to the next in 4th intervals, not progressing any higher than the 3rd fret.

As simple as this looks, focus on producing a great tone and achieving clear separation between each note. Play it slowly and get it sounding smooth before gradually increasing the tempo. We're playing 1/4 notes to begin with, so 90-100bpm would be a good tempo to start with.

Exercise 2

Here is a variation on the basic pattern. After playing the first 4th interval, we return to the first note we played and move up a half step each time. We're now playing in 1/8th notes, so 60-70bpm would be a good starting tempo.

Exercise 3

Here's a more difficult variation on the pattern of Exercise 2. Here we are mixing 1/16th and 1/8th notes, which breaks up the pattern rhythmically and makes it less predictable. I suggest pulling the tempo back to 50bpm on the metronome as your starting point. Our goal is rhythmic accuracy, great tone and great time.

Exercise 4

Var. 2

This exercise takes the previous variation as its template but plays it using 1/8th note triplets. Around 60bpm is a good starting tempo for this one.

Exercise 5

Var. 3

The final variation takes us back to our original pattern but this time we're playing it using 1/8th note triplets, like the previous exercise.

This time, because the notes are arranged in 4ths, it's a little harder to "hear" the triplets to begin with. If you find this difficult, try accenting the first note of every triplet group by plucking it slightly harder than the rest. This should make the triplet patterns pop out a little more.

Exercise 6

Var. 4

3. String Crossing – Part 2

This exercise builds on the previous idea. This time, we're playing a string crossing nine-note phrase, which launches from notes on the bottom string and ascends the fretboard in half steps.

This is a great drill for ensuring that we're playing notes cleanly and with good separation, while playing the whole phrase smoothly and in time. The patterns are arranged in 1/8th notes and the exercise is in 6/4 time signature. I've written out the phrases up to the 12th fret but continue ascending as far as you can.

Exercise 7

Simile -------

4. String Crossing with Rhythmic Variation

We started our string crossing drills by playing two adjacent strings, then three. Now, we're crossing four strings as we ascend in half step intervals.

The first part of this exercise is simpler than the second, as it follows a two-bar pattern played in 1/4 notes. The second part is more challenging because, although it has the same note pattern, it's played in 6/8 time with constantly changing rhythmic variations.

Exercise 8

Now for the second part. Watch out for the challenging 1/16th note rhythms that are harder to execute in 6/8!

Exercise 9

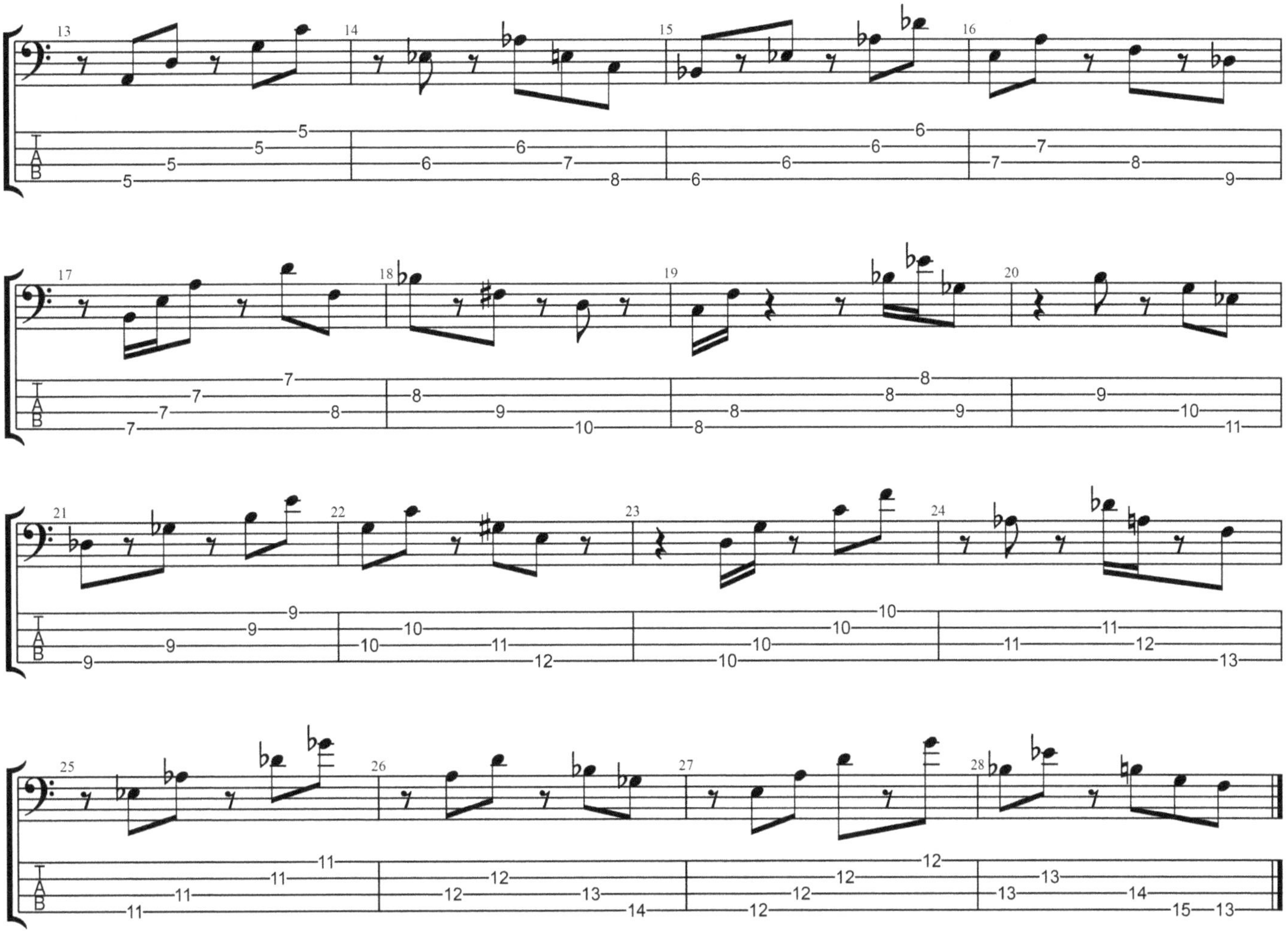

5. Lyric Etude: String Crossing with 4ths

Here's an etude I wrote that includes 4th interval movements and string crossing. It shows how the skills we've been drilling can be put to practice in a real piece of music.

Have a listen to the audio before attempting the piece, because there are lots of dynamic variations here, and it's meant to be played as expressively as possible.

If you've practiced your string crossing drills thoroughly, you should be able to focus less on technique and more on making the music musical! Remember, our ultimate goal is for our technique to become automatic, so that the only thing we're focused on is making expressive music.

Exercise 10

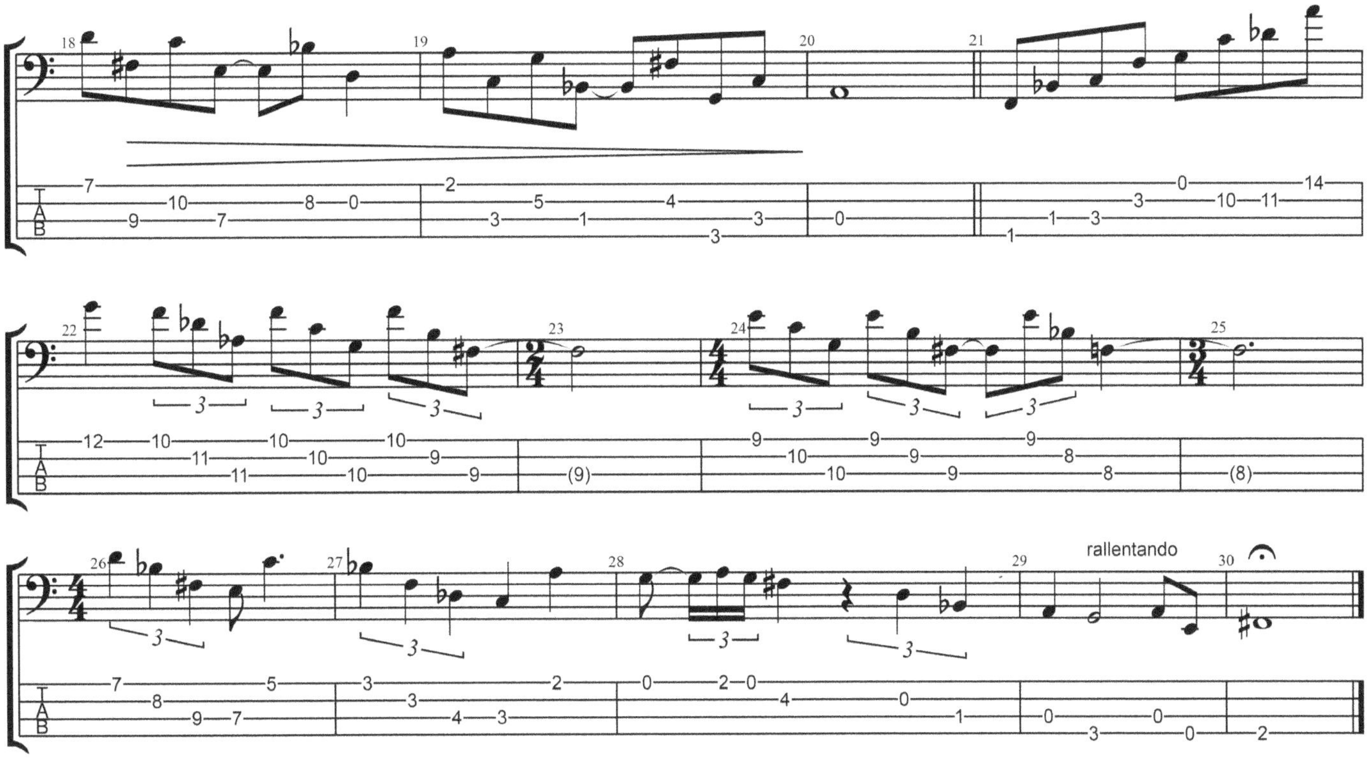
rallentando

6. Bebop Vocabulary for String Crossing Over an F Blues

To conclude this piece of work, here is an etude played over a blues in F. It focuses on playing bebop vocabulary, arranged so that it also provides a string crossing workout. It also contains lots of useful phrases that you can learn, add to your musical vocabulary, and adapt to other keys.

Exercise 11

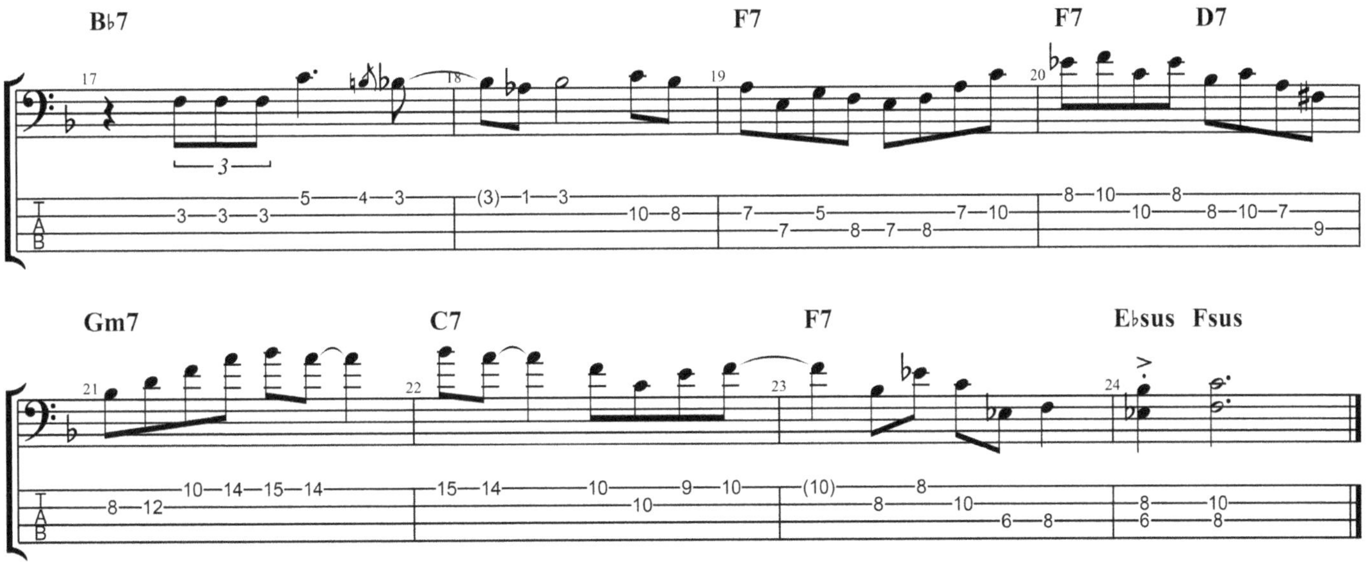
B♭7
F7
F7
D7
Gm7
C7
F7
E♭sus
Fsus

7. Bass Ostinatos

Playing bass ostinatos is a skill that is rarely taught or practiced, so I wanted to cover that skill in this book. Often, in contemporary jazz, the band will play a repeating rhythmic figure (*ostinato*) while the drummer or another instrumentalist takes a solo. At the time of writing, I'm in the middle of a tour with Dave Weckl and Joey Calderazzo, and this is exactly what Joey and I do while Dave takes a drum solo.

Although the idea seems simple on the surface, if you're playing with a great drummer who can really manipulate time and plays a lot of shifting polyrhythms, it can take a great deal of concentration to keep the ostinato figure rock solid.

In this series of short exercises, I'll give you some accented rhythms to work on. Because we're not playing along with a live drummer, the challenge here is to keep the rhythm tight and play in the pocket while increasing the tempo. Even if you don't often find yourself in a situation where you're playing to a live drum solo, these exercises are great on their own for improving your timing.

This first exercise is based around the well-known Cuban rhythm, the *2–3 rumba clave*. If you've ever listened to great Cuban musicians play, you may have noticed that they tap their feet to the rhythm of the clave (not the 1/4 or 1/2 note beat like most musicians). The bass rhythm then changes according to the clave rhythm of the pulse. The bass player never plays the clave rhythm itself, but is expected to know what rhythm to play for each clave.

Exercise 12 lays out the underlying clave rhythm.

Ostinato Rhythm 1: 2-3 Rumba Clave

Exercise 12

Exercise 13 shows what the bassist should play over the 2-3 rumba clave.

Exercise 13

Abakwa/Bembe Rhythm

The Abakwa rhythm or Bembe clave is a polyrhythmic Afro-Cuban pattern that fits into a 6/8 rhythm. This rhythmic feel has its roots in West Africa, but it can be used to spice up blues, funk and jazz.

Exercise 14 shows how to count this rhythm.

Exercise 14

Exercise 15 shows what the bass should play over this syncopated rhythm and we play it at increasing tempos.

Exercise 15

Straight 1/16th Note Funk

Next, we'll look at some funk rhythms, for those times when you want to play ostinato figures on a funk/fusion gig.

First, listen to the audio example, then work through this exercise played in straight 1/16th notes.

Exercise 16

Swing 1/16th Note Funk

Now let's play the same bassline, but this time with a swing feel. Here we are playing the notes as 1/16th note triplets.

Exercise 17

Medium Swing – Elvin Jones Style

I imagine this next exercise being played over a typical Elvin Jones-type drum break. Here, rather than using punchy accents, the bass notes are allowed to ring, almost creating a drone, though we are still playing certain accents.

Exercise 18

Part 2 – Fretboard Knowledge

8. Warm-up Workout: Connecting Triad Shapes in Lower Positions

We start this section of the book with a warm-up drill that focuses on connecting triad shapes and 7th arpeggios in the lower zone of the neck. It's another exercise that is contained within the first four-to-five fret zone, and is a great exercise for learning (and testing) our ability to play through multiple key centers in a single zone of the neck.

This exercise comes in five parts. First, we will drill minor and major triads, then dominant 7 arpeggios, then we'll play a walking bassline, and finally some bebop vocabulary.

Exercise 19 takes us through a series of minor triads moving through the Circle of Fifths without leaving the first four frets.

Set your metronome to around 70bpm for this exercise, but before you play it, take some time to play each triad shape in isolation and think about the notes and the sound of each chord.

Over time, we want to be able to visualize each triad before we play it. Add this drill to your practice routine and aim to be able to play it, in due course, without reading the notation.

Exercise 19

Now let's repeat the exercise, this time playing major triads.

Exercise 20

We'll apply the same concept again, but in this exercise we're playing dominant 7 arpeggios.

Exercise 21

We can immediately apply our knowledge of working with triads/arpeggios in one zone of the neck by playing or soloing over changes.

Exercise 22 is a D Minor blues. In this exercise we play a slow, 1/4 note walking bassline over the changes. The bassline is constructed entirely from chord tones – there are no chromatic approach notes here.

Rather than begin on the root note of the first chord, however, we start on the lowest available chord tone on the bottom string, which happens to be an F (the b3 of Dm7). Then we spell out the blues changes, moving from chord to chord in the same region of the neck.

Exercise 22

Building further on this idea, here is a practice etude that is a solo played over similar D Minor blues changes. The etude uses bebop vocabulary, so approach notes are now allowed, but the concept remains the same: the entire solo is contained within the first five frets.

If you keep working diligently on the earlier drills we've covered, you'll begin to visualize the triad and arpeggios shapes for each chord within the zone. These will then become the "skeleton" frameworks around which you can build melodic phrases, adding approach notes to target the chord tones.

Exercise 23

Bebop Vocabulary on a D Minor Blues

9. Wide Interval Workout

This exercise will train your ability to use the full range of your instrument to play notes related to a simple triad inversion.

It's a workout based on intervals of a 5th. Bars 1-4 illustrate the pattern we'll use. Using this pattern as our template, we'll ascend the neck chromatically on the bottom string.

In bar one, a C major triad is played in first inversion (3 1 5), so that we begin from the lowest available chord tone. Once we've played the 5th of the triad, we then continue ascending in 5th intervals. Then we descend the exact same sequence of notes.

Over time, this exercise will help your visualization of where chord tones are located across the neck and give you a system to quickly locate them. It will also improve your ability to hear intervals.

Finally, it's also a good string crossing exercise in itself, which includes some string skipping, and it's a long exercise, so it's useful for building stamina too!

Exercise 24

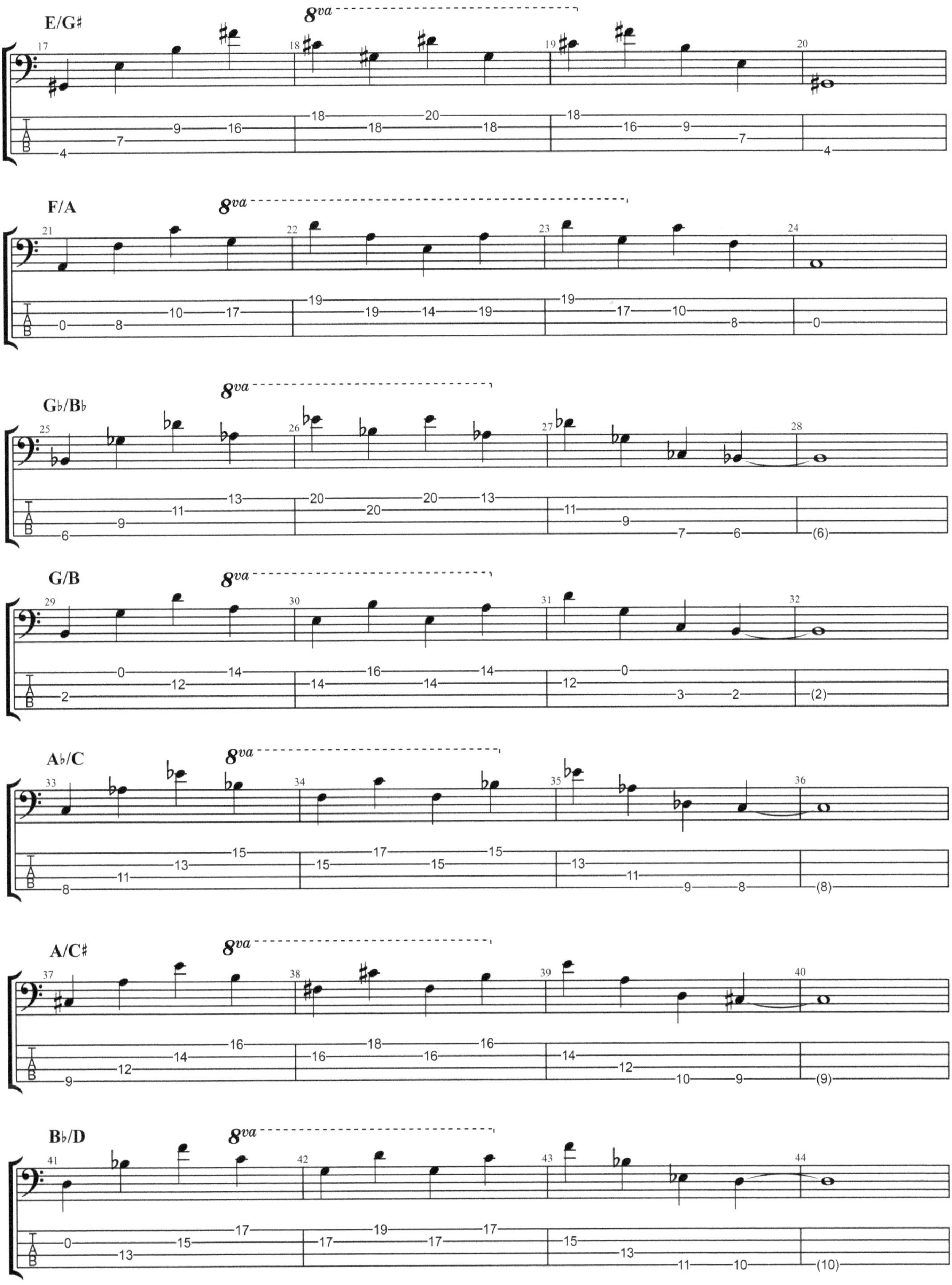
E/G♯
8va
F/A
8va
G♭/B♭
8va
G/B
8va
A♭/C
8va
A/C♯
8va
B♭/D
8va

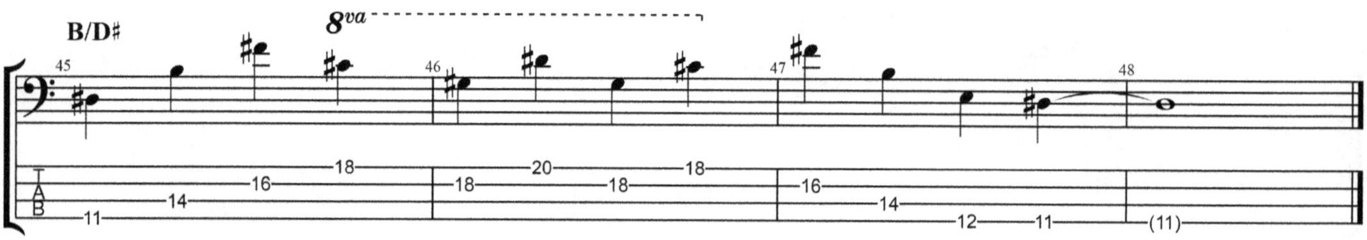
B/D♯
8va
45
46
47
48
T
A
B
11
14
16
18
18
20
18
18
16
14
12
11
(11)

10. Combining Arpeggios

This exercise helps to further develop the skill of connecting chord changes by moving from triad to triad using the nearest available note in the next triad each time, while still moving in the same direction – whether ascending or descending.

This takes a lot of thought and practice to achieve – it's something I continue to work on! But it will help to train your visualization of each arpeggio's layout on the fretboard.

We could play an idea like this using a predictable chord progression, such as a I – vi – ii – V sequence, but here the progression is *unpredictable* so we can't simply rely on our ears. We have to know both the notes that form each arpeggio *and* where those notes are located on the fretboard.

The exercise first moves through a series of major triads, then minor triads. Once again, the aim is to use the full range of the instrument to execute the triads.

Exercise 25

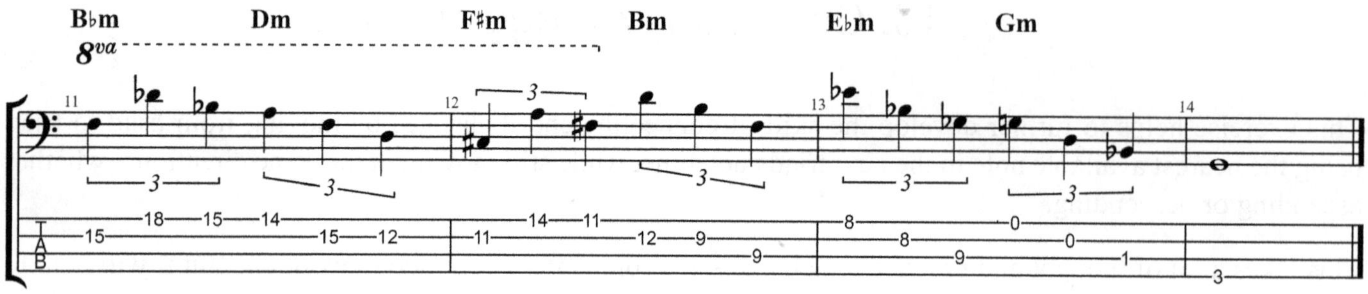
B♭m
Dm
F♯m
Bm
E♭m
Gm
8va

11. Triad Combinations Chord Tone Soloing Etude

Exercise 26 is a 32-bar etude that focuses on chord tone movements. It's a musical exercise that connects a series of triads or 7th chords using the nearest available note.

Exercise 26

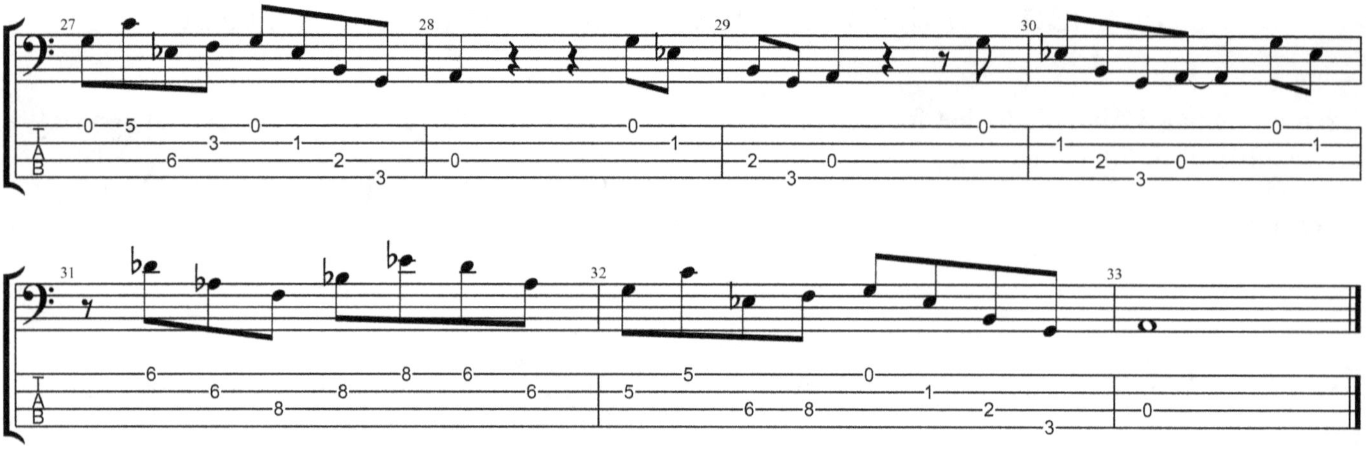

12. Connecting Parallel Major 7 Sounds Moving in Minor Thirds

For the most part, tunes in the jazz standard repertoire follow fairly predictable chord cadences and changes. In that context, it's easy to become familiar with navigating sequences such as the ii – V – I progression, because those tunes are full of them!

A lot of contemporary jazz, however, features modal ideas, where the chords shift up or down in specific intervals. Sometimes, these chords will retain the same quality i.e., all major chords moving in intervallic jumps, or all minor chords, etc. This means it's good to develop the skill of navigating modal chord changes of the same type, so that when we encounter them in a piece of music we already have some vocabulary, ready to be used.

This series of exercises gives you some melodic jazz language over a series of major 7 chords. Each chord is separated by a descending minor 3rd interval. The minor 3rd shift is one of the most popular ideas in modern jazz. Work through the exercises individually, then play all the exercises together as a single etude.

First we move from Cmaj7, down a minor 3rd to Amaj7, then to F#maj7 and Ebmaj7.

Exercise 27

Let's play through those changes again, but extend the patterns to two bars of each chord. This means we need to work a little harder to create an interesting melody. Varying the rhythm of our phrases is a great tool in this context.

Exercise 28

Now let's repeat that process from a new starting point: Dbmaj7. Again, the chords are descending in minor 3rds.

Exercise 29

Let's extend the sequence with two bars for each chord.

Exercise 30

Now let's change the sequence again and descend in minor 3rds from Dmaj7.

Exercise 31

Next, the extended version of the same chord changes.

Exercise 32

You may have noticed that every time we completed a cycle of changes, we then moved up a half step.

So, the exercises have moved us through descending minor 3rds from Cmaj7, Dbmaj7 and Dmaj7. There is no better way to really learn the fretboard than being forced to play through sequences we wouldn't normally go to.

Here is the full major 7 etude that links together all the previous exercises. Aim to learn it well enough to play along with the audio.

Exercise 33

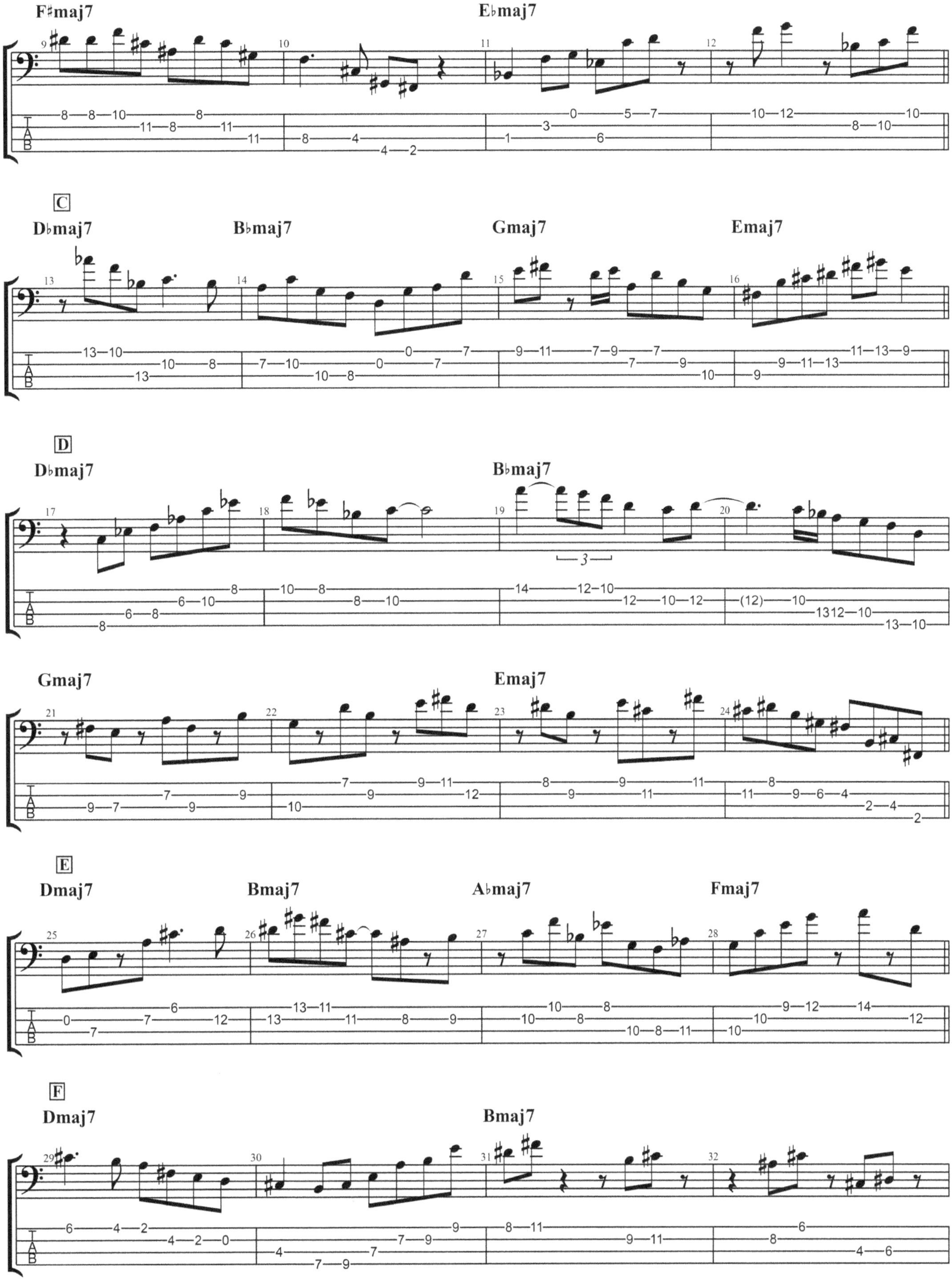
F♯maj7
E♭maj7
C
D♭maj7
B♭maj7
Gmaj7
Emaj7
D
D♭maj7
B♭maj7
Gmaj7
Emaj7
E
Dmaj7
Bmaj7
A♭maj7
Fmaj7
F
Dmaj7
Bmaj7

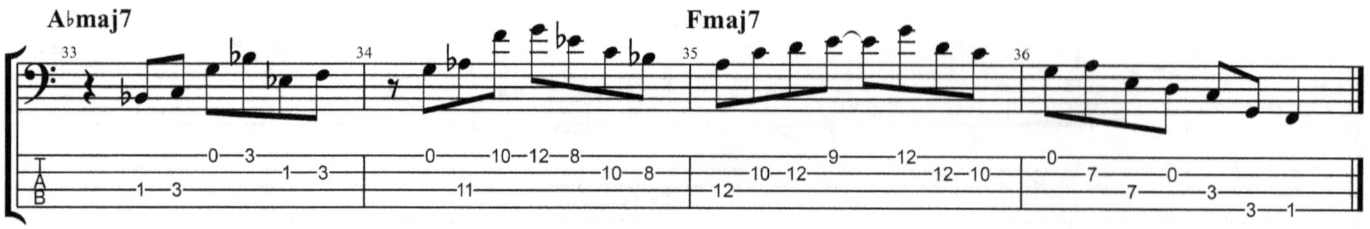
A♭maj7
Fmaj7

13. Major 9 Arpeggio Etude

Let's focus on major chord sounds for a while longer. The next exercise is a jazz etude based on the concept of soloing over just major 9 chords.

The major 9 is a mainstay of modern jazz chord voicings and is often used as a more open sounding alternative to the major 7. This etude will help you to develop some vocabulary as you practice forming melodic phrases over the chord.

At the same time, this is another test of fretboard visualization. We will move through a sequence of major 9s, shifting down a whole step each time e.g., Fmaj9 – Ebmaj9 – Dbmaj9 etc.

The first time we run through this sequence we'll play two bars for each chord. The second time through, we'll play just one bar per chord. Like the other exercises we've worked on, the aim is to use as much of the range of the instrument as possible.

In this exercise, I'm viewing each chord as Lydian. In other words, chord IV in the harmonized major parent scale. E.g., Fmaj9 is chord IV in the key of C Major, so for this chord the notes will come from the F Lydian scale (identical to a C Major scale beginning and ending on the note F). For the Ebmaj9 chord, we'll use Eb Lydian (parent scale: Bb Major), and so on.

Exercise 34

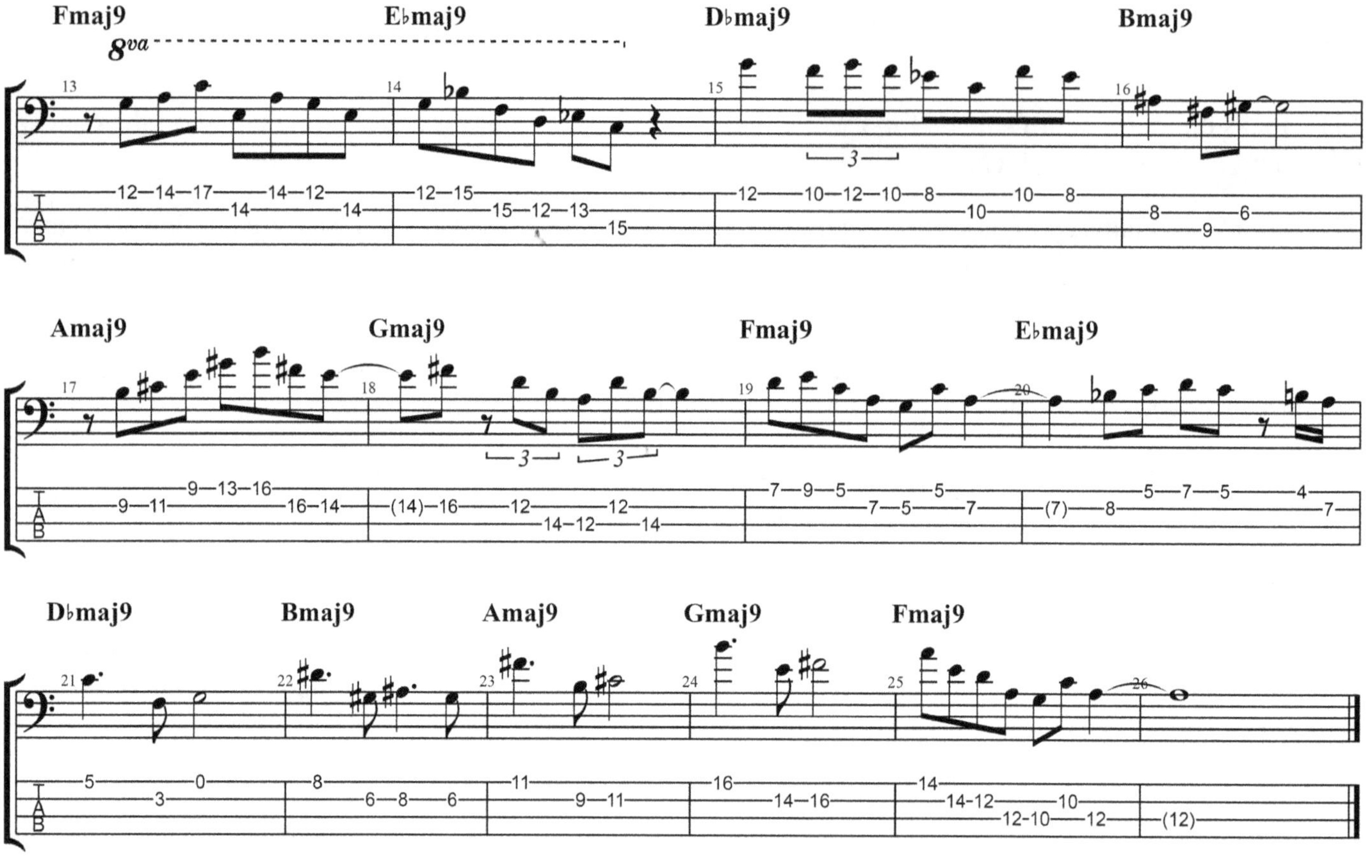
Fmaj9
E♭maj9
D♭maj9
Bmaj9
8va
Amaj9
Gmaj9
Fmaj9
E♭maj9
D♭maj9
Bmaj9
Amaj9
Gmaj9
Fmaj9

14. Connecting Minor 7 Sounds Moving in Minor Thirds

Now we'll turn our attention to connecting modal minor sounds across the fretboard. This is the minor 7 version of the major 7 exercise we just played. We'll use the same tonal centers as before, but now we'll play minor 7 chords descending in minor 3rds.

Once again, the aim of this exercise is to develop some melodic vocabulary around chords of the same quality moving in minor 3rds.

First, Cm7 moving down a minor 3rd to Am7, then F#m7 and Ebm7.

Exercise 35

Now let's extend that pattern so that we have to create two-bar melodic phrases for each chord.

Exercise 36

Now the tonal center shifts up a half step and we begin on Dbmaj7, then descend in minor 3rds.

Exercise 37

Next, we extend the chord changes.

Exercise 38

Now we move up another half step to repeat the exercise with new melodic vocabulary.

Exercise 39

And, finally, we extend those bars.

Exercise 40

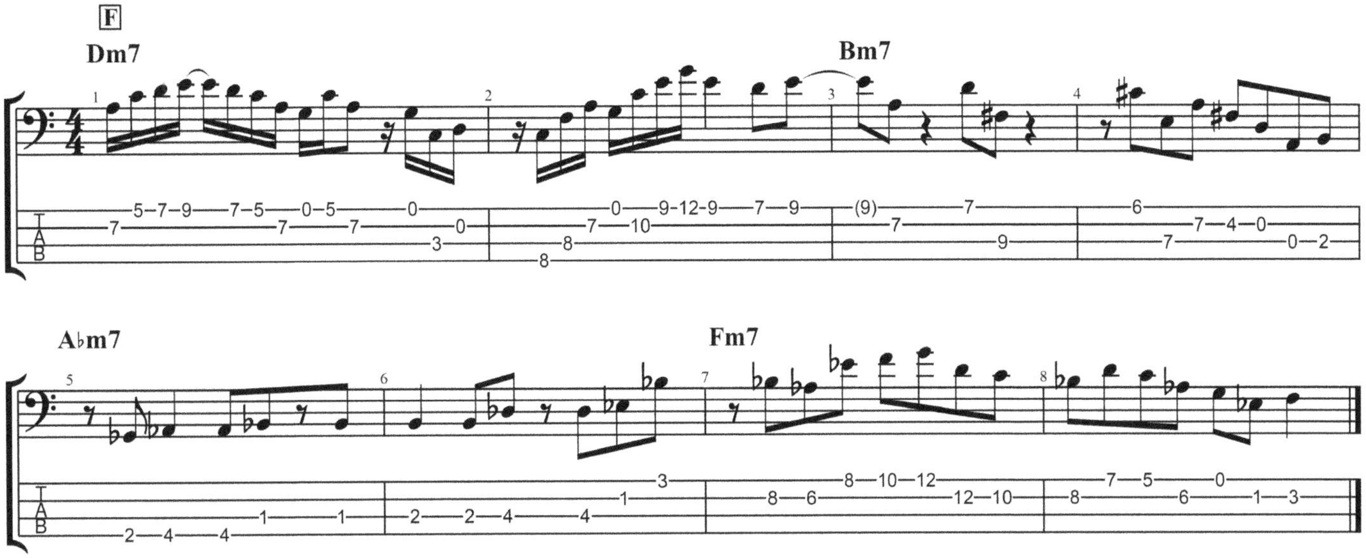

15. Modal Exercises with Syncopation

This exercise is really 12 exercises in 1, with each part tackling a different scale or mode.

Its purpose is twofold:

First, it's an exercise in reading rhythms. The rhythms are challenging here, combining both triplet and 1/16th note syncopations.

Second, it shows how we can apply scales in a melodic way, rather than approaching them in a pattern-based, sequential way.

The latter approach obviously has its uses, but it's much more liberating to be able to jump into a scale at any point and create a melodic phrase.

NB: This exercise is *not* for learning the scales, you'll need to put in that work on your own. There are a number of different free fretboard mapping tools online that will help you to lay out the scale across the fretboard for visual reference. Rather, this is all about mastering the geography of the scale with melodic application.

If you take all 12 parts and combine them into one exercise, you'll see that the scales move sequentially through the Circle of Fourths.

Exercise 41 – C Bebop Scale

Exercise 42 – F Melodic Minor

F Melodic Minor

Exercise 43 – Bb Lydian Augmented

Bb Lydian Augmented (G Melodic Minor)

Exercise 44 – Eb Lydian Dominant

Eb Lydian Dominant (Bb Melodic Minor)

Exercise 45 – Ab Half-Whole Diminished

Ab Diminished (Half - Whole)

Exercise 46 – Db Major

Exercise 47 – Gb Major

Exercise 48 – B Major

B Major

Exercise 49 – E Harmonic Minor

E Harmonic Minor

Exercise 50 – A Harmonic Major

A Harmonic Major

Exercise 51 – D Harmonic Minor

D Harmonic Minor

Exercise 52 – G Augmented

Part 3 – Diminished, Whole Tone, Augmented Sounds & Tetrachords

16. Descending Diminished Arpeggios

As we begin to look at more advanced concepts, we start with an exercise to help you to learn every diminished position. It provides a useful pattern that can be applied when playing over altered dominant chords and uses two diminished 7 arpeggios separated by a whole step (Cdim7 and Ddim7 or Bdim7 and Dbdim7).

The repeating pattern of 1/8th notes starts on a root note, moves up to the b3, down to the bb7 and down to the b5 on the first arpeggio, then drops a half step into the next arpeggio to play the b3, down to the root, up to the b5 and up to the bb7.

Assuming a bass neck of 20 frets, this exercise starts at the highest fret and works its way down to the lowest note available. Working out a comfortable fingering for this exercise is key, so that you can move smoothly between positions. Play through it very slowly and find an economical fingering that works for you, minimizing any awkward position changes.

Exercise 53

17. Whole Tone Scale Cells

This fretboard workout uses a similar concept to the previous exercise, but here we shift between two whole tone scales a minor 3rd apart (A Whole Tone and C Whole Tone).

In bar one, beginning with the open A string, we play the first three notes of A Whole Tone (A, B, C#), then drop back a half step to play the first three notes of C Whole Tone (C, D, E).

Now on the D string, we drop back another half step and pick up where we left off with A Whole Tone, playing its Eb, F and G notes. Then we jump back into C Whole Tone to play its F#, G# and A# notes.

In bar two, we move away from the string crossing pattern of bar one, and instead just ascend on the top string, but the pattern of notes is identical to before. Playing the sequence along one string takes us from the 2nd all the way up to the 15th fret.

Mixing approaches and alternating between *horizontal* and *vertical* approaches is a great way of ensuring we can both hear and visualize the intervals we want to play.

In bars 3-4, the entire sequence of bars 1-2 is reversed to descend the fretboard. In subsequent bars, the variations are created by changing the order of the notes.

In bars 7-8, we change the order of the melodic *cells* for the first time, so don't get caught out by that! Then we switch back in bars 9-10.

We switch up the order again for the remainder of the exercise, where the aim is to play the cells arranged like triads rather than in a linear, scalic fashion.

These cellular phrases sound great when played at a faster tempo and a good practical application of them would be to solo over an altered dominant chord (E.g., try soloing over an A7#5 chord vamp using alternate A Whole Tone and C Whole Tone cells).

Exercise 54

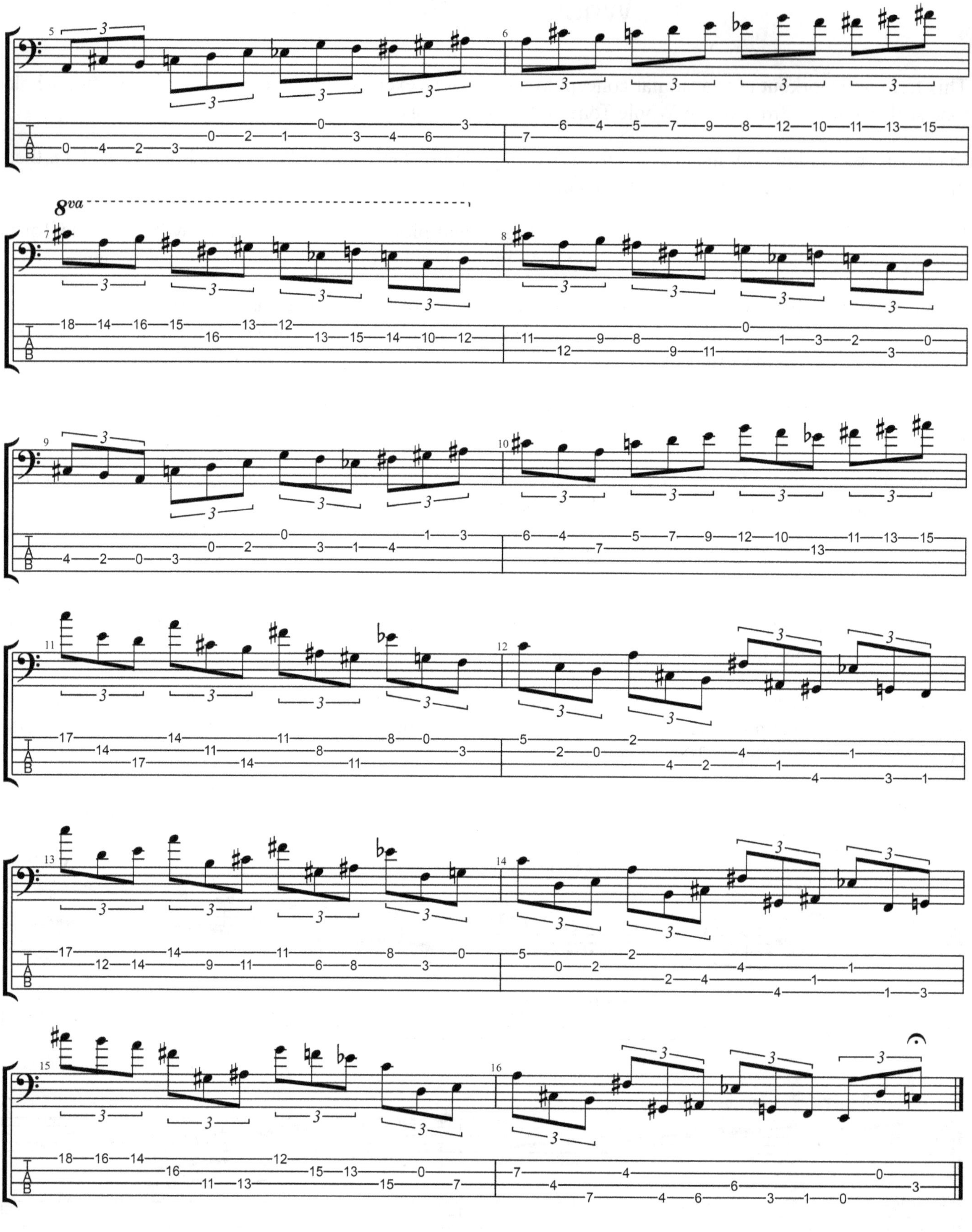
8va

18. Whole Tone Sounds – Scales & Triads

I have been listening to the music of John Coltrane and Wayne Shorter all my life and have always been fascinated by the augmented harmony approach of these giants, and especially the way in which McCoy Tyner played on their records. I wrote these whole tone exercises/etudes to capture the essence of that sound.

McCoy played a lot of interesting intervallic material that used whole tone sounds and I thought this might help bass players (especially me) to achieve more flexibility in playing these intervallic shapes.

First, an exercise that highlights the fact that by using just two whole tone scales, C and A, we can cover all twelve keys.

Exercise 55

With this principle in mind, play through the follows two etudes that capture the sound of the A and C Whole Tone scales.

19. A Whole Tone Scale

Using the A Whole Tone scale, in this etude we're taking six notes from the scale and working on variations, playing mostly with 1/4 notes, 1/8th notes and 1/8th note triplets.

Exercise 56

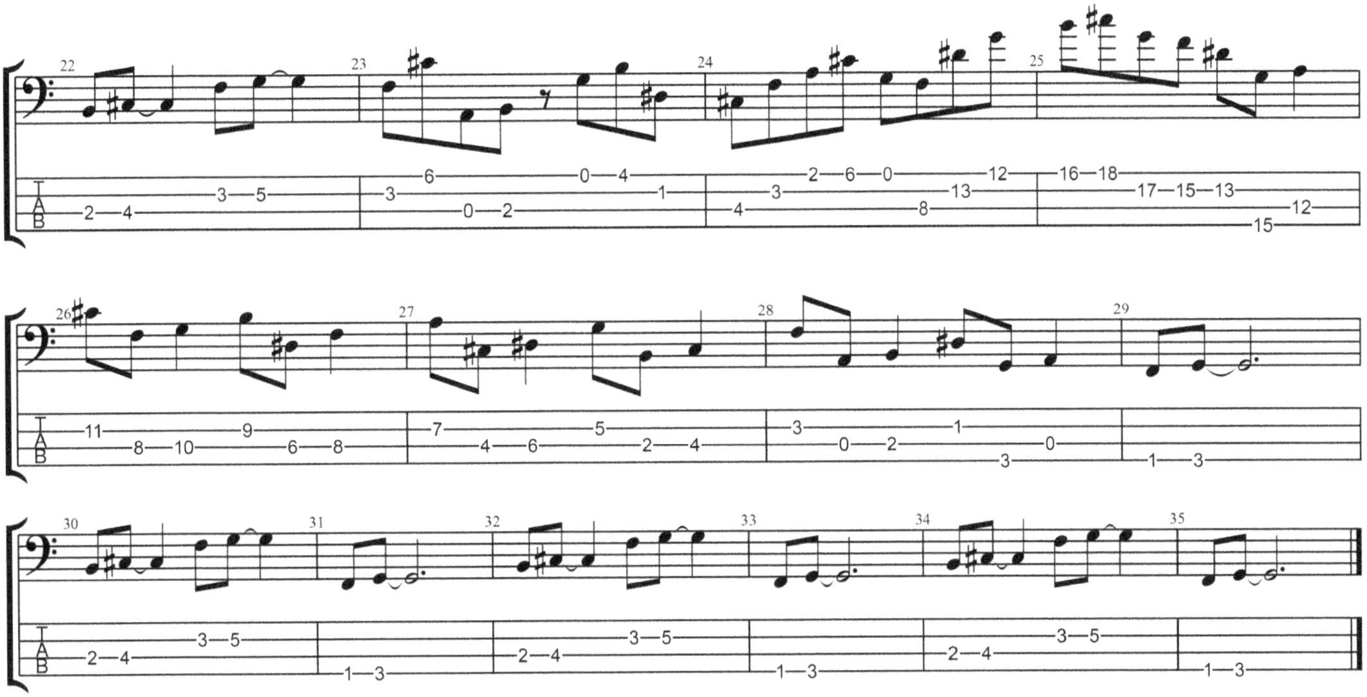

20. C Whole Tone Scale

This etude is written using the C Whole Tone scale, which has the notes C, D, E, F#, G#, A#.

The nature of the whole tone scale means that one scale can be used to play over Major 7+5 chords launching from each degree of the scale. In other words, we can play C Whole Tone over C7+5, D7+5, E7+5, F#7+5, G#7+5 and A#7+5 chords.

Exercise 57

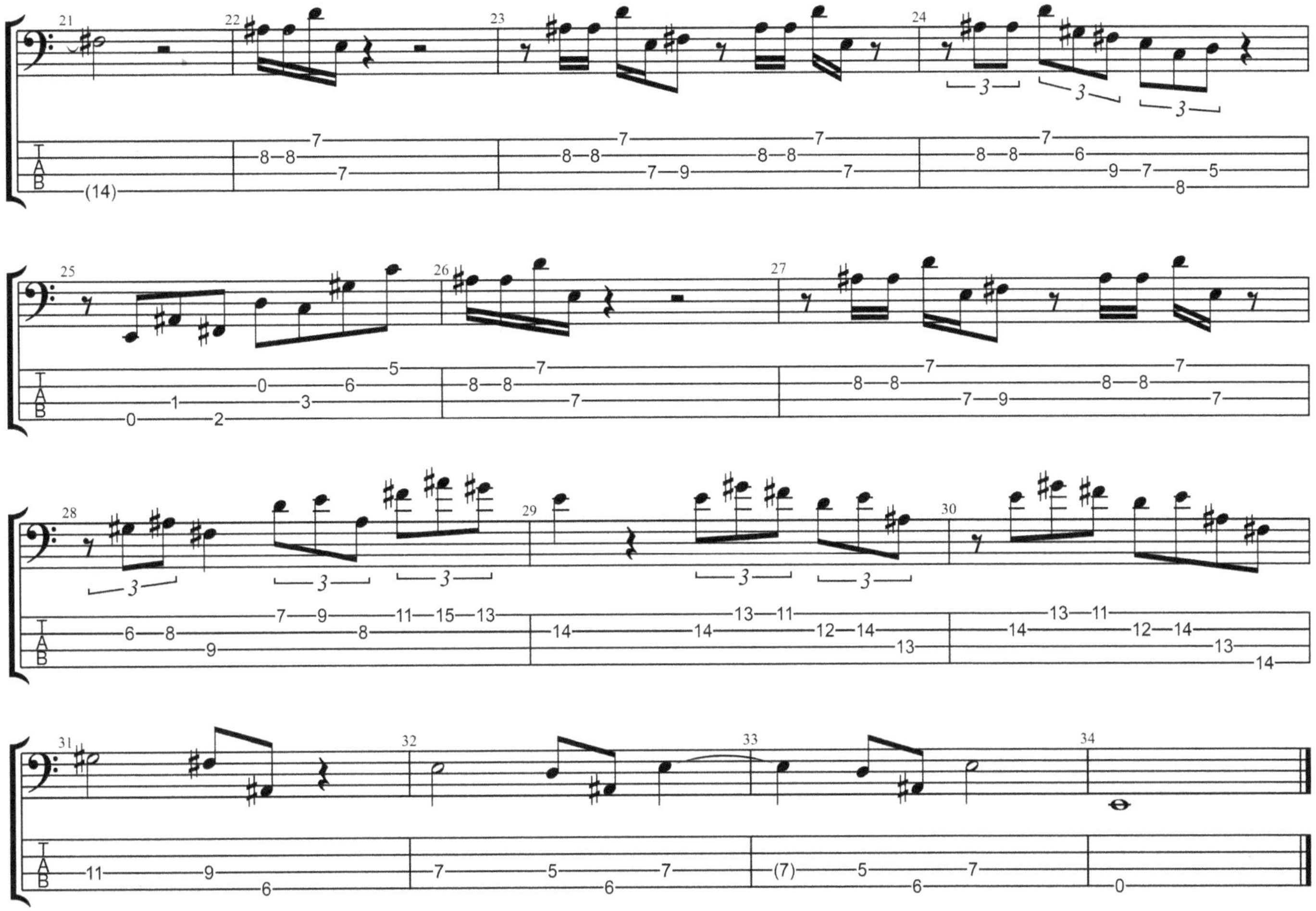

21. Augmented Hexatonic Scale Exercise

I wanted to cover the augmented sound as it is so prevalent in modern jazz compositions. Another approach to playing over Major 7+5 chords is the Augmented Hexatonic Scale, formed by combining three major triads, each separated by a major 3rd interval.

If we begin on C, that structure gives us the notes:

C, Eb, E, G, Ab, B

You may notice that as well as containing C, E and Ab major triads, that set of pitches also gives us C, E and Ab *minor* triads.

The Augmented Hexatonic Scale is a mode of "limited transpositions". In other words, it has just four modes and those modes cover all twelve keys. This first exercise can be used for reference as we play through the major and minor triads in each mode.

Exercise 58

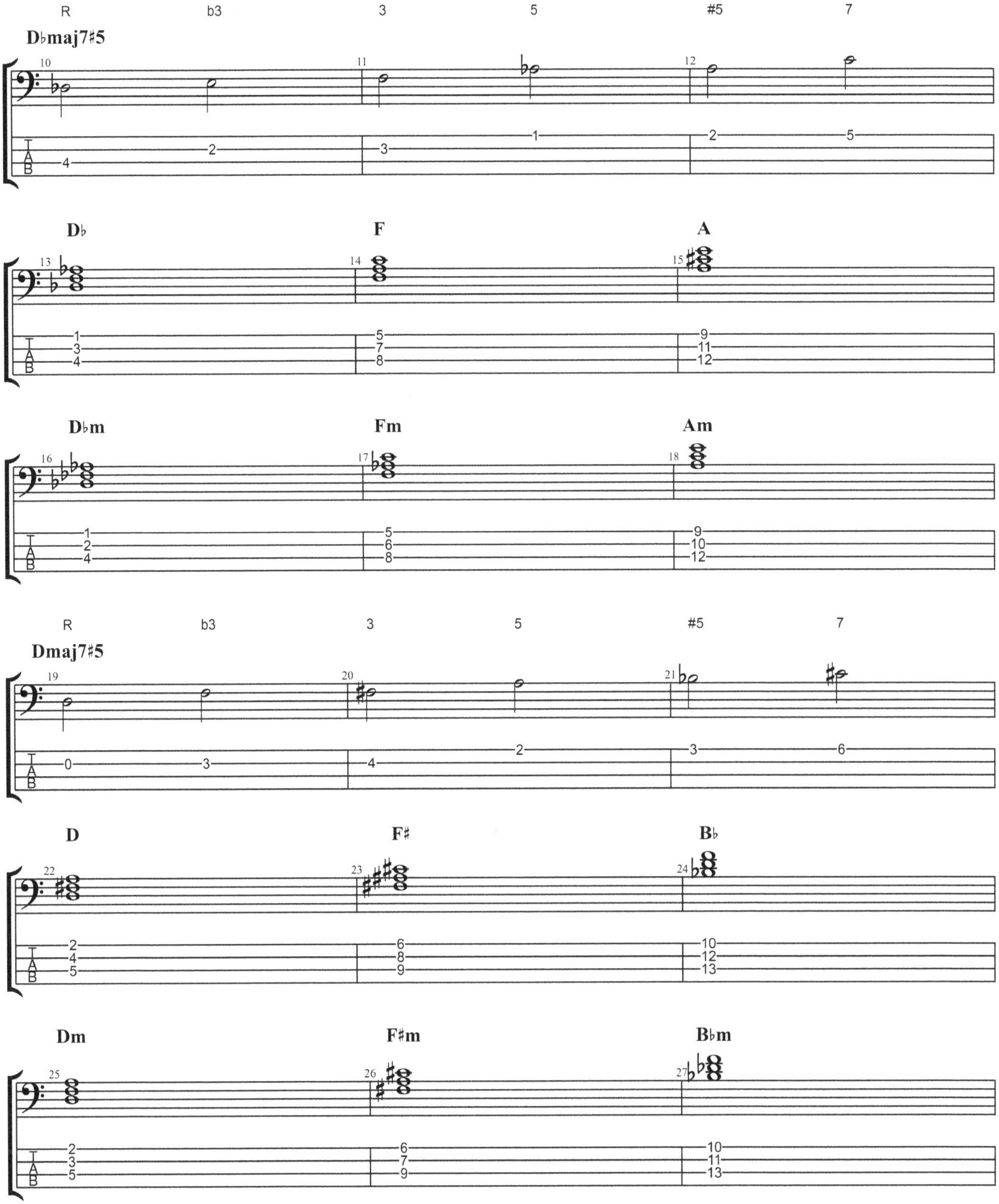
R b3 3 5 #5 7
D♭maj7♯5
D♭ F A
D♭m Fm Am
R b3 3 5 #5 7
Dmaj7♯5
D F♯ B♭
Dm F♯m B♭m

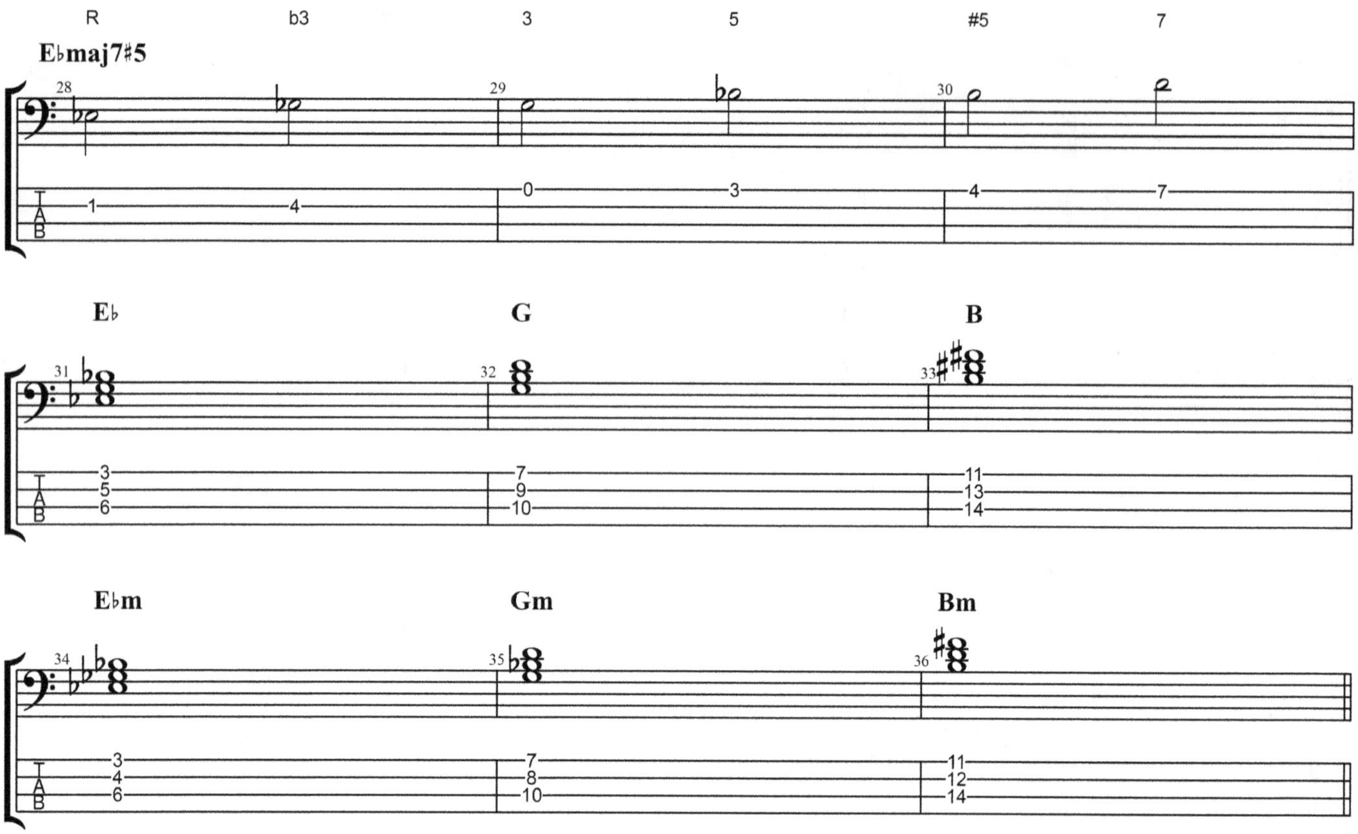
R b3 3 5 #5 7
E♭maj7♯5
E♭
G
B
E♭m
Gm
Bm

22. C Augmented Hexatonic Etude Over Cmaj7#5

Next, we'll explore this scale further by playing an etude using the C Augmented Hexatonic over a Cmaj7#5 chord.

Exercise 59

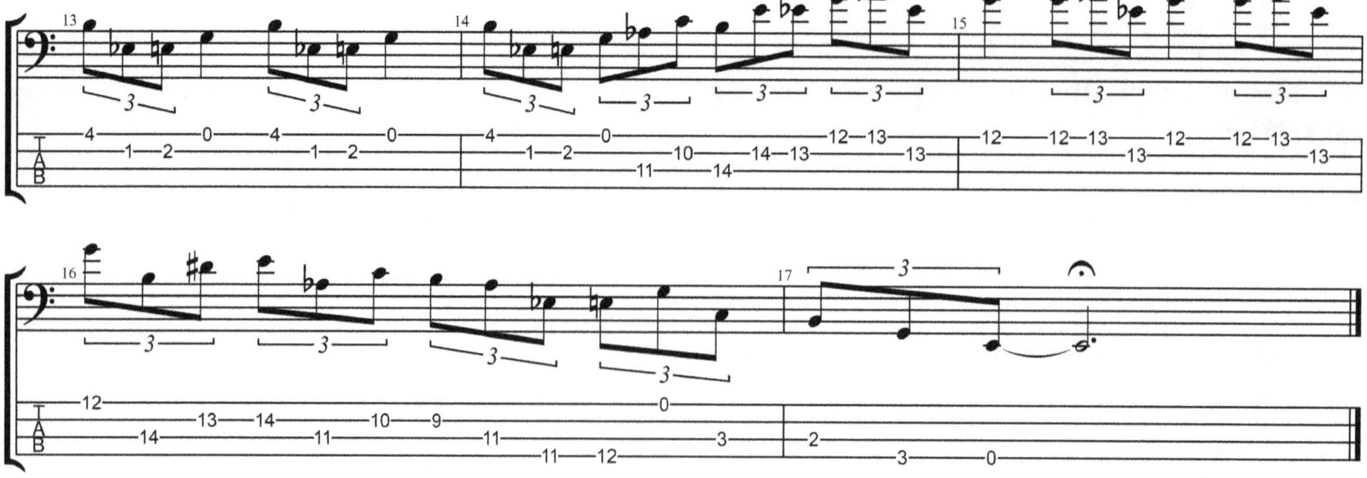

23. Db Augmented Hexatonic Etude Over Dbmaj7#5

Let's do the same thing playing Db Augmented Hexatonic Scale over a Dbmaj7#5 chord.

Exercise 60

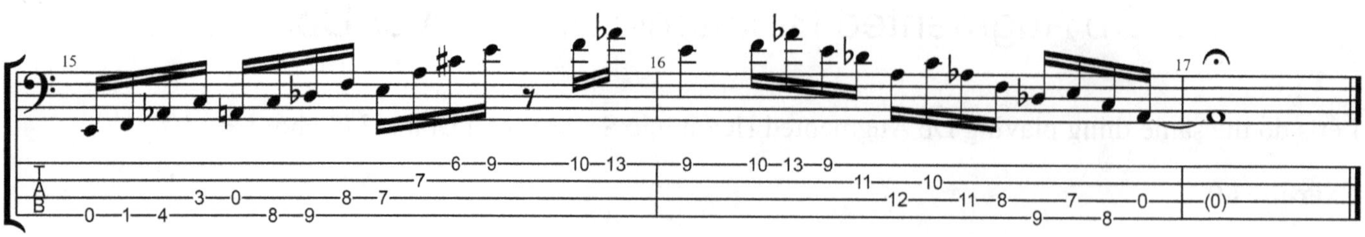

24. D Augmented Hexatonic Etude Over Dmaj7#5

Next, the D Augmented Hexatonic Scale over a Dmaj7#5 chord.

Exercise 61

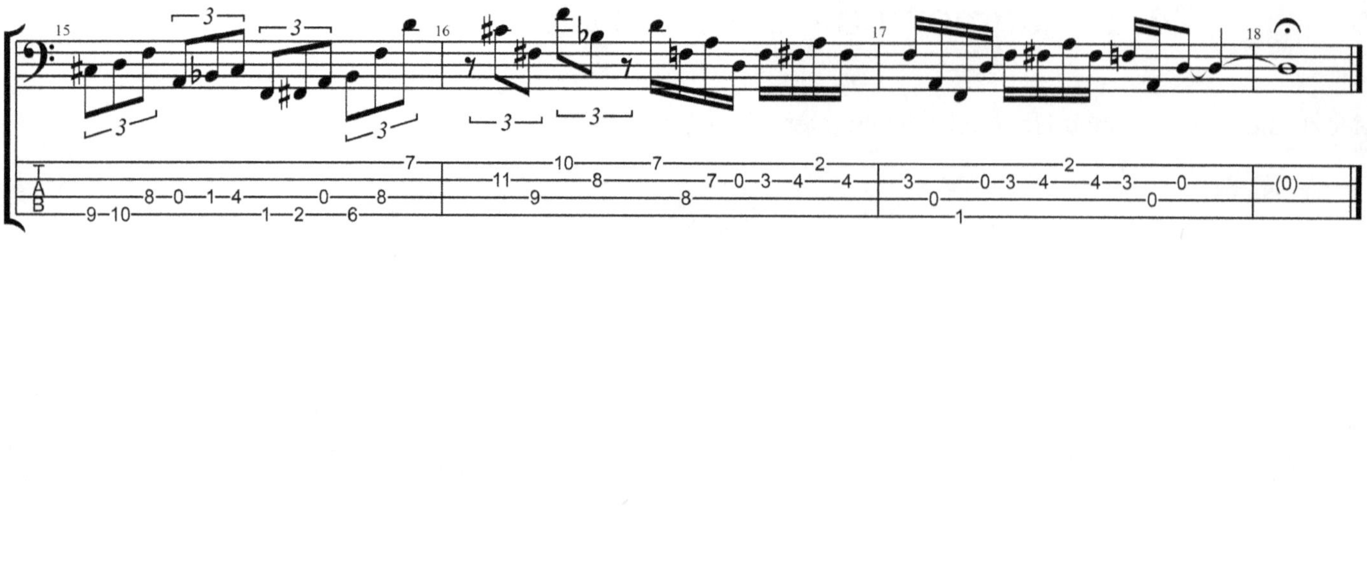

25. Eb Augmented Hexatonic Etude Over Ebmaj7#5

And, finally, the Eb Augmented Hexatonic Scale over a Ebmaj7#5 chord.

Exercise 62

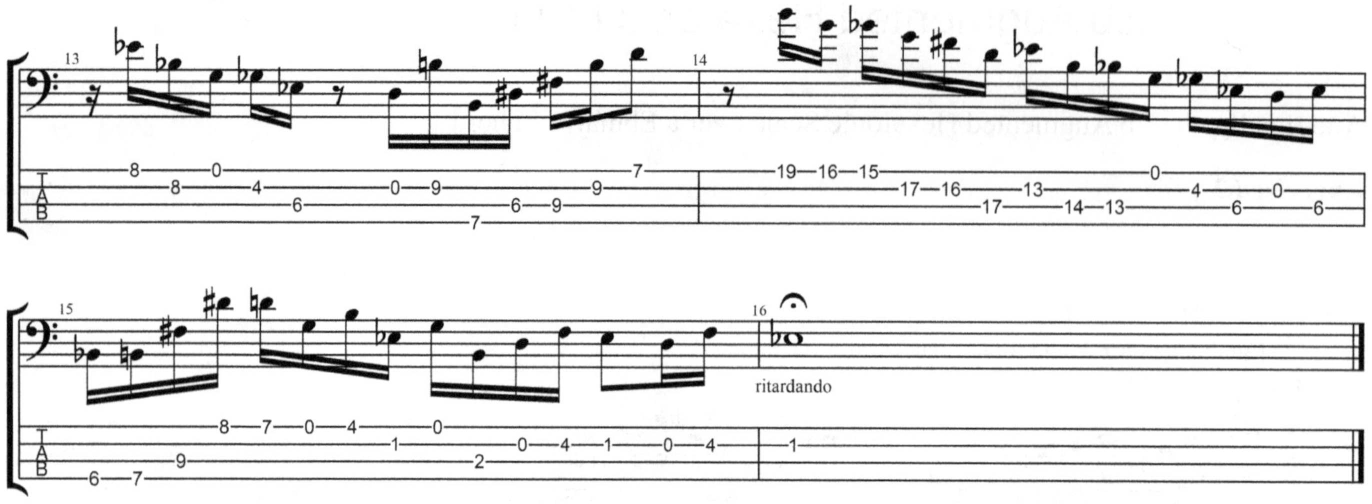
ritardando

26. Descending Major 7#11s with the 15th Interval

Here is an exercise we bassists need! When practicing arpeggios, it's very tempting to always ascend from the root, so here is an exercise in which we only descend. Furthermore, it helps us to hear and utilize some very interesting intervals.

I describe this exercise as a major 7#11 with the 15th interval. That is the outcome of the series of intervals you're about to play. Let me explain...

All the arpeggios here are played descending. Let's flip around the notes in bar one below for a moment to understand what's happening.

The idea is to start on a C note and play a major 3rd interval (C to E). Next we play a minor 3rd interval (E to G. Then we play a major 3rd interval again (G to B), then another minor 3rd, and so on. We alternate this pattern to create an eight note arpeggio.

The result of stacking these alternating major and minor 3rd intervals is a beautiful chord structure which can be described as a Cmaj7#11+15.

The first four notes spell a Cmaj7 (C, E, G, B) but as we continue stacking alternate major and minor 3rds, we add the pitches of D, F#, A and C# to create a more complex chord. This process introduces the 9th, 13th, #11 and b9 intervals into the chord.

Interestingly, if you play this chord on piano, even though the lowest note is a C and the highest note a C#, in context that high 15th interval doesn't sound dissonant.

Another way of understanding and describing what we've created is that we've stacked a Dmaj7 on top of a Cmaj7. Each arpeggio is described this way on the notation below to help you understand each grouping of notes, but the core idea is that we are extending the sound of a major 7 chord to add colorful tensions, in the way that most contemporary modern jazz pianists do.

This exercise gives us a technical workout – because it means having to visualize different arpeggios in the upper register of the bass – and opens our ears to new sounds at the same time. It also gives us some cool options to play whenever we see a major 7#11 chord on a lead sheet.

Exercise 63

A

Dmaj7/Cmaj7　　　　　**Fmaj7/E♭maj7**　　　　　**Gmaj7/Fmaj7**

Amaj7/Gmaj7　　　　　**Bmaj7/Amaj7**　　　　　**D♭maj7/Bmaj7**

Cmaj7/B♭maj7　　　　　**B♭maj7/A♭maj7**　　　　　**A♭maj7/G♭maj7**

F♯maj7/Emaj7　　　　　**Emaj7/Dmaj7**　　　　　**E♭maj7/D♭maj7**

B

Fmaj7/E♭maj7　　　　　**E♭maj7/D♭maj7**　　　　　**D♭maj7/Bmaj7**

78

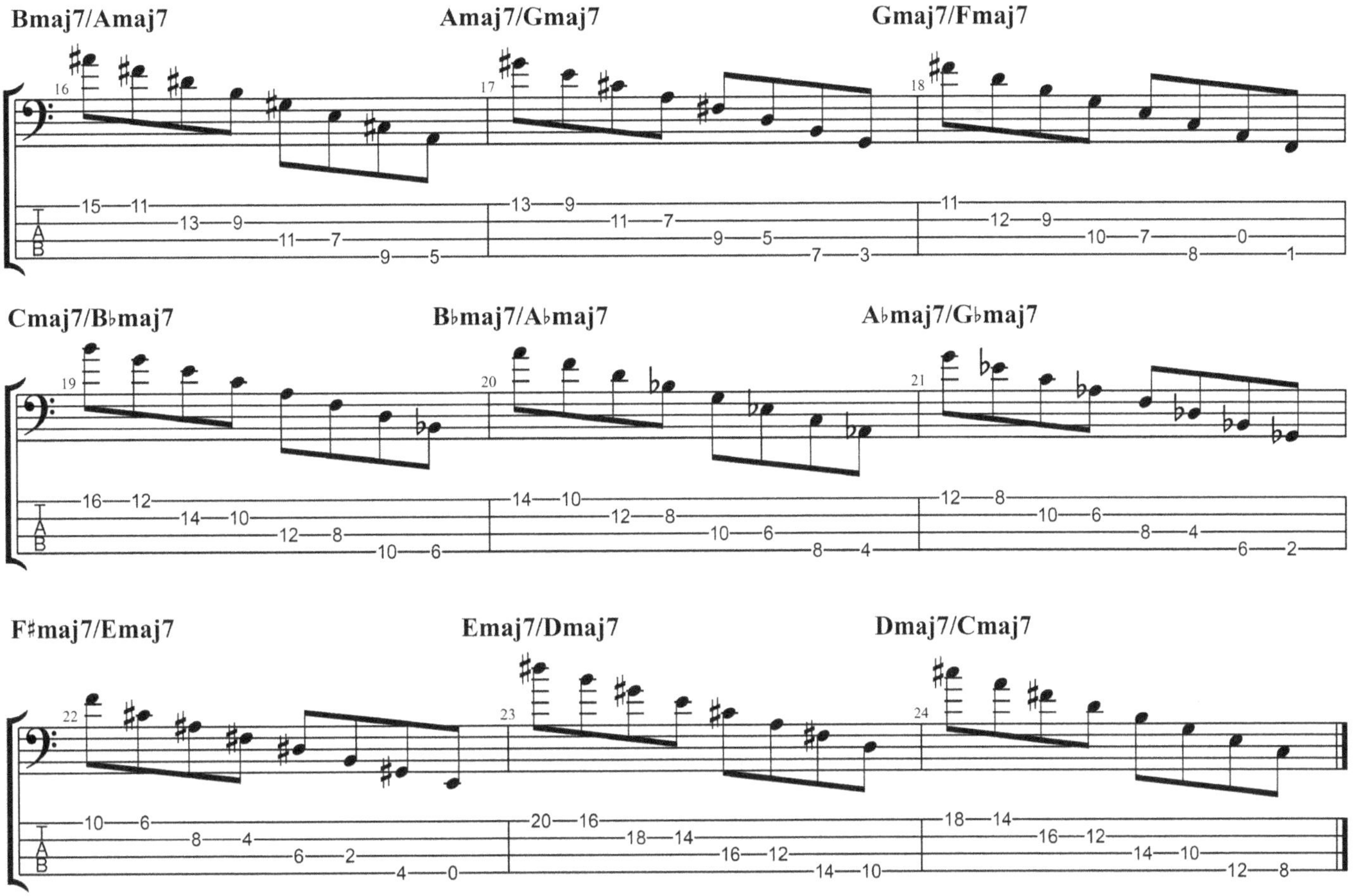
Bmaj7/Amaj7
Amaj7/Gmaj7
Gmaj7/Fmaj7
Cmaj7/B♭maj7
B♭maj7/A♭maj7
A♭maj7/G♭maj7
F♯maj7/Emaj7
Emaj7/Dmaj7
Dmaj7/Cmaj7

27. Bartok-Inspired Tetrachord Shapes

When I was playing with Chick Corea, he got me listening to the music of Bartók, who was one of the early explorers of modal music. Bartók used a technique that he called *polymodal chromaticism*, where he would construct artificial scales based on superimposing one mode onto another, or the notes of one chord on top of another, a little like the tetrachord idea we've just explored.

But in Bartók's music, you'll often hear chords or scale fragments of *different* tonalities overlapping or stacked on one another, such as Major paired with Phrygian, or Lydian and Locrian. Joining together tetrachords of different qualities was a central part of this approach.

In the previous exercise we saw that we can combine two major 7 chords, but we can also stack tetrachords of different qualities to create an extended harmony. For example, stacking an Fm6 arpeggio on top of a Bb7 arpeggio is an idea that goes all the way back to Charlie Parker. We can also combine two four-note sequences from different scales to form a new hybrid scale containing some interesting tensions.

John Coltrane explored the idea of combining tetrachords extensively in his music, which can be heard particularly in his landmark recording of *Giant Steps*, in which he plays a series of four-note patterns to navigate the tune's unusual chord changes.

The idea of layering or stacking harmony has been used by many great jazz pianists, but there was no better exponent than Chick Corea. Chick often used Bartók-like tetrachord shapes in all kinds of chromatic ways and was incredibly adept at applying them. Sometimes, he might play just the first three notes of a major chord ascending, then descend a different major or minor chord. On the face of it, this sounds like a very simple technique, but often Chick would play these things in two hands, octaves apart, and the resulting sound was very expansive and orchestral.

Advanced Tetrachords – A Crash Course

Let's look again at the idea of stacking tetrachords to form new harmonic structures, this time from a scalic rather than chordal point of view. Let's take the C Major scale.

The first four-note pattern, known as the *lower tetrachord*, uses the scale notes C, D, E, F.

The second four-note pattern, known as the *upper tetrachord*, uses the notes G, A, B, C.

Combined, they make up an eight-note C Major scale with the root note repeated in the higher octave.

Where things get interesting is that the C Major upper tetrachord, contains notes identical to those in a G Major lower tetrachord (G, A, B, C), which promotes the idea of endlessly overlapping harmonies.

In modern jazz improvisation, it has become common to ascend/descend tetrachords combining tonalities.

For example, we could play C, D, E, F (C Major lower tetrachord) and G, A, **Bb**, C. Here, we've altered one note of the C Major upper tetrachord to change it into the lower tetrachord of G Minor.

Or we could play C, D, E, **F#** then G, A, B, C.

Technically, this tetrachord combination creates the C Lydian scale, but the point of the tetrachord approach is to break down scales into more manageable structures and focus on simple four-note building blocks.

In practical terms, this approach means that we can look at a progression that moves from one chord to another, and see different possibilities for creating extended harmony and tensions. We can also use the space *between* the chords to explore all kinds of chromatic possibilities for navigating from one chord to the next. It allows us to weave in and out of harmonies, and it teaches us better voice leading as we seek to create tension and release.

The following etude explores this idea. It also contains some complex rhythmic variations and changes of time signature.

Exercise 64

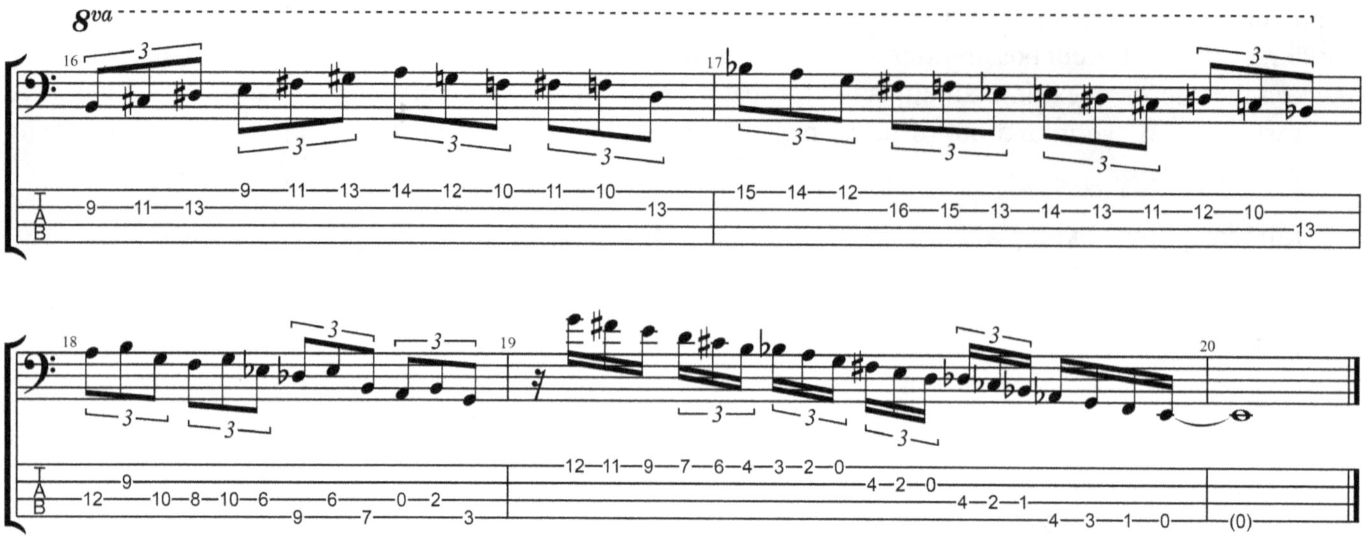
8va

Conclusion

We've covered a lot of ground in this book, looking at many different skills that the modern bassist needs to develop – a combination of technique and musical knowledge.

To get the most out of the exercises and etudes in this book, don't view them as a task to complete, but rather a toolkit for growth. They were crafted to target specific areas of bass technique: harmonic understanding, fretboard visualization, groove and feel, alongside technical skills such as mastering string crossing and using the full range of the bass guitar.

In your next practice session, pick one technical drill and one musical drill. It could be string crossing variations paired with the etude for connecting minor 7 arpeggios in minor 3rd movements. Use the string crossing drills as a warm-up, starting slowly, aiming for clean and precise playing. Once warmed up, use the minor 7 etude to work on your visualization skills and fretboard knowledge. Work on different ideas each week.

The modular design of the book allows you to focus on specific goals you have for your playing and tailor your practice time accordingly. Always use a metronome when practicing, as developing your inner sense of time is one of the most critical skills you'll need to elevate your playing. Also make tone a central focus. Even the most intricate harmonic ideas will lose their value if they are not executed cleanly and with musicality.

As you revisit and become more comfortable with the material in the book, work at achieving higher tempos or adding dynamics and rhythmic articulation to suit your own tastes. Many exercises, especially the whole tone, diminished and augmented ideas, are meant to stretch your harmonic thinking, so don't rush these. Sit with them and experiment, and try incorporating these ideas into your improvisations or compositions.

With consistent, focused practice, you'll find that this collection of exercises and etudes will not just improve your playing, they'll reshape how you think about the music we all love.

John Patitucci